The
*Beginning of a Woman*
Global Ministry

# SPIRITUAL WARFARE PRAYERS

## For the Joshua Generation

By Rev. Lautrina Irene Patterson

*"Verily I say unto you, whatsoever ye shall bind on earth
shall be bound in heaven; and whatsoever ye shall loose
on earth shall be loosed in heaven." Matthew 18:18*

authorHOUSE®

*AuthorHouse™*
*1663 Liberty Drive*
*Bloomington, IN 47403*
*www.authorhouse.com*
*Phone: 1 (800) 839-8640*

*Cover photography by Cibola Henderson of CibolaShoots Photography*

*Published by AuthorHouse 02/14/2017*

*ISBN: 978-1-5246-5353-8 (sc)*
*ISBN: 978-1-5246-5352-1 (e)*

*Library of Congress Control Number: 2016920580*

*Print information available on the last page.*

# DEDICATION

This book is dedicated to *The Beginning of a Woman Global Ministry.* To the thousands of men, women, boys, and girls who will be delivered by the believing and speaking the prayers offered in this book. If you have not accepted Jesus Christ as your Lord and Savior, take a moment and pray the sinners' prayer. If you do not belong to a local church have a minister come in agreement with you for your deliverance. Contact the ministry if you need assistance. I speak healing, deliverance, and blessings into your life.

AMEN

# ACKNOWLEDGEMENTS

With special thanks:
To the Father, the Son, and the Holy Spirit
To my Pastor, Dr. Warren H. Stewart Sr.

> *Thank you for your support and prayers. You believed in me and saw something divine in me that I could not see. You are not just my pastor, you are my friend. I love and appreciate you.*

To my Mother, Dorothy May Patterson
To my children
To my church family (FIBC)
To my spiritual mothers, Wylene and Evette
To my family in L.A
To my friend, Star

# CONTENTS

# INTRODUCTION

God offers you the "Children's Bread" through this book based upon His Word. Jesus defines the "Children's Bread" as deliverance. The scriptures below record a conversation of a gentile believer and Jesus discussing the condition of her daughter who is ill. Here, Jesus presents deliverance as the Children's Bread. And these signs and wonders follow them that believe... Mark 16:17

> *"Behold, a woman of Canaan came out of the same coasts, and cried unto him, saying, Have mercy on me, O Lord, thou Son of David; my daughter is grievously vexed with a devil. Then came she and worshipped him, saying, Lord, help me. But he answered and said, It is not meet to take the children's bread, and to cast it to dogs. And she said, Truth, Lord: yet the dogs eat of the crumbs which fall from their masters' table. Then Jesus answered and said unto her, O woman, great is thy faith: be it unto thee even as thou wilt. And her daughter was made whole from that very hour." Matthew 15: 21-28*

As children of God, deliverance is a part of our covenant or inheritance.

> *"Giving thanks unto the Father, which hath made us meet to be partakers of the inheritance of the saints in light." Colossians 1: 12*

There are some things that may keep you from being delivered through the prayers that are written inside of this book.

1.  Not being saved. If you are not saved and you would like to be, pray this prayer to assure your salvation.

    *Dear Jesus, forgive me of my sins. I believe you are the Son of God and you took the punishment for my sins on the cross. Please come into my heart, be my Lord and my Savior. Amen*

2.  Not binding the Strong Man

    *"Or else how can one enter into a strong man's house, and spoil his goods, except he first bind the strong man? and then he will spoil his house." Matthew 12:29*

The Strong Man can be any evil spirit (whether it is sin, unbelief, fear etc.) who considers your body his home. We must first bind the strong man. Evil spirits must be bound in the name of Jesus and loosed from you to receive your deliverance using the prayers written in this book by the power of the Holy Spirit. Read Matthew chapter 16 verse 19.

Pray this prayer.

> *Heavenly Father, I humble myself before you in worship and praise. I plead the blood of Jesus over my life, my family, church, city, nation, finances, home, heart, emotions, mind, body, and my soul. I realize that I am the temple of the Holy Spirit.*
>
> *Satan, I command you and all your evil spirits of curses, sickness, sin, pride, passivity, ungodly soul ties, occultism, fear, embarrassment, unbelief, lack of desire, unforgiveness, and confusion in my life today to be bound and gone. I bind the stronghold of every demonic spirit that is against my body and mind in the name of Jesus Christ. I loose you.*

*I loose the peace, joy and righteousness of the Holy Spirit to rule and reign in my heart, soul and mind.*

*I surrender my heart, mind, body and soul to you today, Jesus. You have not given me the spirit of fear but of power and love and a sound mind. I resist the spirit of fear, doubt and worry because I have authority over the enemy in the name of Jesus.*

*I claim absolute victory over the forces of darkness. I bind the devil and command him to flee.*

*Heavenly Father, fill me with your love, patience, kindness, goodness, faithfulness, gentleness, self-control, and prosperity for the glory of God. Holy Spirit I ask that Christ may dwell in my heart by faith and I am rooted and grounded in the love of God.*

*In the name of Jesus,*

*AMEN*

# ABANDONMENT

Most gracious Father, I come to you asking that you would forgive me of all known and unknown sins. I come, Lord God, surrendering my every thought unto you today. I come desiring to be free of the strongholds over my life that have left me feeling abandoned, isolated, deserted, lonely, neglected, rejected, separated, self-pity, or victimized, in the name of Jesus. Your word says in Hebrews chapter 13:5 you will never leave me or forsake me. Lord, I believe.

> *"And the LORD, he it is that doth go before thee; he will be with thee, he will not fail thee, neither forsake thee: fear not, neither be dismayed." Deuteronomy 31:8*

Lord God, I come ready to forgive the person and people whom I held responsible for my feelings. I bind up family curses and the curses on single parent homes. I forgive growing up as an orphan by every circumstance, being adopted into an abusive home, growing up not knowing one or both parents, being raised by grandparents, experiencing divorce and feeling it was my fault, and suffering because of my parents' sins in the name of Jesus.

Father, I bind demon grouping spirits of insecurity, passivity of body and emotions in the name of Jesus. I loose the peace of God. I ask that Father, fill my soul with the fruit of the Holy Spirit. The Spirit that seeks the highest good for others, the Spirit that is slow to speak and slow to anger, the Spirit that is generous and open hearted, the Spirit that is merciful, sweet and tender, the Spirit that is contentment and unity between people, the Spirit of gladness that is not based on circumstance, the Spirit that is dependable, loyal, and full of trust.

Lord, I put on the full armor of God – especially the helmet of salvation that will protect my mind from doubting God's saving work for me.

In the name of Jesus I pray,

AMEN

# ABORTION AFTERMATH

Lord, I acknowledge you as the Triune God – the Creator, Man, and Comforter. I thank you for the blood of Jesus that cleanses me from all sin and unrighteousness. Today, Holy Spirit I call on you to lead, guide, and direct me in all truth and righteousness. Father God in the Name of Jesus I ask that you forgive me of all known and unknown sins, of all sins of omission and commission, of all sins committed intentionally and unintentionally, of all sins of thoughts, words, and deeds. Heavenly Father, I ask you to forgive me for consenting to abort my unborn child(ren). In the name of Jesus, I bind up the spirit of death with its fruit of abortion and murder. I loose it. I loose life and life more abundantly in me. I come against the curse of Rachel, depression, guilt, sickness, fear, condemnation, sorrow, grief, weeping, and mourning.

The effects of Abortion Aftermath *(like: suicidal thoughts and attempts, alienation from family and friends, feeling 'numb,' not able to feel joy, isolating myself from others to avoid discussing the abortion experience with them, difficulty concentrating, anger toward self, or the child's father, or others involved in the abortion decision, sleep disorders, abortion-related nightmares, flashbacks or even hearing the sound of a baby crying, alcohol and drug problems, anniversary reactions of grief or depression on the date of the abortion or the baby's expected due date and feelings of depression, guilt, shame, fear, condemnation, sorrow, grief, weeping, and mourning)* I command you to come out of my life right now and stay out forever. I ask for the love of God to come into my life and to comfort me with the Holy Spirit.

*"Who forgiveth all thine iniquities; who healeth all thy diseases; Who redeemeth thy life from destruction; who*

3

*crowneth thee with lovingkindness and tender mercies."*
*Psalm 103:3, 4*

Heavenly Father, forgive my sins, heal my diseases, and deliver my life from destruction. Replace depression with joy. Replace guilt with peace. Replace sickness with healing. Replace fear with faith. Replace condemnation with love. Replace sorrow with goodness. Replace weeping with rejoicing. Replace mourning with patience and kindness. Do this through the power of Jesus' shed blood and through your divine Holy Spirit.

In the name of Jesus,

AMEN

# ABORTION CONTEMPLATING

Our Father – the Creator, the Healer, the Redeemer – I thank you for the blood of Jesus, shed on Calvary, that cleanses me from all sin and unrighteousness. Today I call on the power of the Holy Spirit to forgive me, heal me and deliver me from the snare of the enemy. Lead me, guide me, and direct me in all truth and righteousness.

> *"And thou shalt not let any of thy seed [children] pass through the fire to Molech, neither shalt thou profane the name of thy God: I am the LORD." Leviticus 18:21*

Heavenly Father, I ask that you forgive me for everything I have said or thought that was contrary to your will for my life. I ask that you forgive me in the precious name of Jesus for contemplating having an abortion. I have allowed the spirit of abortion (murder), the curse of Molech (sacrificing children to idols), rejection, fear, suicide, the curse of rejection from the womb, to enter within me against your will. In the name of Jesus I bind and cast out these spirits and the spirit of rejection, fear, and suicide. I break the curse of abortion contemplation, Molech, and rejection over this unborn child in the name of Jesus. My child will live and not die!

I ask for your angelic protection to cover my child and replace each evil spirit with the spirit of love, joy, peace, faithfulness, acceptance and goodness. I speak blessings into my child's life. I will love him or her forevermore. I thank you for this blessing. Comfort me and my child, Holy Spirit.

In the powerful name of Jesus,
AMEN

# ADDICTIONS

Heavenly Father, Jesus and Holy Spirit, I come surrendering all – my heart, mind, soul and body. I surrender my past, my future, my addictions and my very life to you today. I admit, Father, that I am addicted to *(name addiction: cocaine, downers, uppers, heroin, marijuana, nonprescription drugs, tranquilizers, alcohol, caffeine, cigarettes, food, computer, gambling, internet, pornography, over spending, sex, sports, television, video games.)*

> *"Bring my soul out of prison, that I may praise thy name: the righteous shall compass me about; for thou shalt deal bountifully with me." Psalm 142:7*

Father, I ask that you would put a shield over my ears so that I may hear your voice speaking to me. Put a guard and shield over my mouth. Father, I ask that you remove the scales from my eyes so that I may see with your eyes. I ask that you would cleanse my body, the temple of the Holy Spirit, and make me pure and holy because my body is not my own. Help me, Lord, to remember when temptation comes that I belong to you.

Lord, forgive me for not coming to you when I didn't know how to deal with my past abuse when I was a child or when I was being molested or raped. Lord, forgive me for not coming to you when I didn't know how to deal with being rejected. Forgive me for not coming to you when I didn't know how to deal with my divorce or with my children, my spouse, my job, my family, my failures, my responsibilities, my grief, my disappointments, my accident, my adoption, my home, my parents, *(list other situations).*

My decisions have affected my body - my teeth, breath, weight, organs, eating, breathing, hygiene and appearance. Jesus, help me, restore me, redeem me, cleanse me, free me, heal me, deliver me and strengthen me. Jesus, break every chain that binds me. Today I humble myself, turn from my wicked ways and seek your face. Lord, lead me, guide me, and direct my path.

In the name of Jesus,
AMEN

# ANGER

Heavenly Father, I come to your throne of grace today seeking your forgiveness for the sins I have committed. Today, I surrender my emotions to you so that you can have complete control over the way I think, feel and act. Lord, go before me send your angel before me to drive out the spirit of anger. Heal my mind from the memories and my body from being violated *(through rape, incest, molestation, physical and or verbal abuse)*. I choose to stop judging myself and forgive the person who sinned against me *(the person's name)*. Lord God, forgive me for every door have I opened that created a demonic entrance into my life: *through books, literature, music, movies, cultic and occult reading, and pornography* during my childhood, youth, teenage years and adult life.

> *"Be ye angry, and sin not: let not the sun go down upon your wrath: Neither give place to the devil." Ephesians 4:26, 27*

Lord, bind up all the anger in my heart that was the result of: *(abandonment, feuding, frustration, hatred, hostility, murder, punishment, rage, resentment, retaliation, revenge, being spoiled, temper tantrums, and violence or death against a family member or friend (name the person).* I no longer give place to the devil. In the name of Jesus, I bind up the spirit of unbelief, mocking, pride, rebellion, bitterness, and violence which have allowed anger in my heart in the name of Jesus. Lord, I rebuke the spirit of anger that has entered into my heart through my unforgiveness, lack of knowledge, bloodlines, relationships and associations, ungodly soul-ties, failures, frustrations, family problems, marital problems, miscarriages, suffering, distresses, and hard times as well as accidents, unfair treatment, poverty, starvation, recession, loss of father or mother, setbacks, mishaps, condemnation, helplessness, and business failures.

Lord, deliver me and set me free me from all that has me bound from of the spirit of anger. Send us your peace that surpasses all understanding to me and my family.

In the name of Jesus,

AMEN

# ABUSE

Lord Jesus Christ, I believe with all my heart that you are the Son of God; you left your throne of glory in heaven and came to earth as a man. You came to heal the broken hearted. Today I receive your healing.

> *"He healeth the broken in heart, and bindeth up their wounds." Psalm 147:3*

I renounce and break free from the sin of abuse which has been passed down through my bloodline, family and culture. I break free from word curses, immoral soul-ties, evil associations, secrets and deception, domination by men or women, and ungodly patterns and cycles, in the name of Jesus. I break free from demonic bondages placed upon me as the result of physical, mental, sexual, verbal, emotional, and spiritual abuse like: *(low self-esteem, fear, confusion, rejection, insanity, forgetful, paranoia, schizophrenia, hysteria, hallucinations, worry, nervousness, self-pity, people pleasing, suicide, and the fear of leaving relationships.)* In the name of Jesus, I confess my sins and I accept your forgiveness.

Lord, people have trespassed against me but you have commanded me to forgive each person who has ever hurt or wronged me. I now make the decision to forgive *(name them: my parents, adoptive parents, boyfriend, girlfriend, husband or wife, family members, enemies, schools, university, ministry, church, pastor, first lady, teacher, mentor, fiancée, deacon, deaconess, bishop, choir director, preacher, minister, laymen, missionaries, office staff)*. Father, I thank you for delivering me from every curse, sin and iniquity that was used against me by the spirit of abuse.

You cause me to be fruitful in all I do. I am successful, I am not a failure. I am the head and not the tail. I am your servant. I put on the full armor of God and choose to walk after the Spirit. Lord, bless and keep me. Thank you, Jesus!

In the name of Jesus,

AMEN

# ANXIETY

Heavenly Father, I come to you just as I am - burdened and heavy laden. I confess the sin of anxiety to you and ask for your forgiveness. Help me turn from this evil spirit that has given me a false sense of responsibility, in the name of Jesus. Satan, the Lord rebukes you.

*"Casting all your care upon him; for he careth for you."* 1 Peter 5:7

Lord I surrender control and cast all of my concerns *(name your concerns like: my children, sickness, finances, divorce, some change in life, my family or friend, singleness, isolation, blocked intimacy, performance, menopause, mental problems, graduations, marriages, ungodly relationships, and infirmities.)* upon you. Worrying about these circumstances has negatively affected my emotions. I have felt *(name the emotions like: fatigue, loneliness heaviness, nervousness, restlessness, weariness, fear, stress, exhaustion or confusion).*

Merciful God, I ask you to take over my emotions, thoughts, burdens, stresses, worries and concerns. Give peace to my heart, mind, body and soul. I give you every situation I've been concerned about, work them out for your glory.

Send me your love, patience, peace, self-control, goodness, faithfulness, gentleness, grace and mercy.

In the precious name of Jesus,

AMEN

# BITTERNESS

Father God, I thank you for your grace and your mercy. I lay every disappointment at your feet so that you can deliver me from the spirit of bitterness. Forgive me, Lord, for allowing the actions and behavior of people like: *(father, mother, sister, brother, church members, friends, ex-boyfriend, ex-girlfriend, teacher, mentors, pastor, ministry leader, ex-pastor, first lady, ex-first lady, professional person, probation officer, country guard, police officer, warden, boss etc.)* to provoke me to anger and cause me to become bitter. Father God, I choose to forgive those people who abused me – emotionally, physically, mentally, sexually, spiritually, and verbally. I forgive those who imprisoned, raped, or tortured me or those I love.

> *"Looking diligently lest any man fail of the grace of God; lest any root of bitterness springing up trouble you, and thereby many be defiled." Hebrews 12:15*

Forgive me, Father God, for defiling others and allowing the things of this world like: *(the Boom and Bust economic cycle, defeat, pressure to succeed, striving, despair, heart break, mental torment, diseases, inadequacy, poverty, sexual perversion, witchcraft, pride, sinful attitudes, lying, slander, tragedy, frustration, family problems, business failures, stumbling blocks, suffering, ill fortune, setbacks, hard times, distress, calamity, mishaps, slumps, cross prayers, curses and rebellion)* to affect me. Satan, you have to flee. I rebuke and let go of the bitterness that was caused by them.

All accusation, blaming, complaining, condemnation, criticalness, gossip, judging, murmuring, ridicule, slander, and unforgiveness have to leave my life now! Lord, I come under complete submission to the

Father, Son and the Holy Spirit. Send your angelic protection to watch over me. Holy Spirit, draw me near.

I ask for your wisdom, knowledge, understanding, revelation and discernment as you begin a good work in me.

In the name of Jesus I pray,

AMEN

# CASTING OUT DEMONS

Heavenly Father, I come to you asking for a special anointing to cast out the demons in (person's name). Lord God, I pray that you would send down your angels to protect me and to seal off any transferring spirits, in the name of Jesus. Holy Spirit, I ask that you would give me discernment in calling out every demon that has demonized or possessed (name the person). Authority is given to me by Jesus Christ who is far above all rule and authority. *(As the Holy Spirit leads you begin to cast out every demon discerned in the name of Jesus.)*

> *"Ye are of God, little children, and have overcome them: because greater is he that is in you, than he that is in the world." 1 John 4:4*

I plead the blood of Jesus over your life and cast out every satanic spirit that has entered into your heart, mind, body, and soul in the name of Jesus. Satan, you do not have permission to speak or hurt this person. I bind you in the name of Jesus and by the power of His blood. You must leave now and may not touch anyone else.

*(Begin to look for deliverance – coughing, drooling, vomiting, belching, yawning, or exhaling.)*

Holy Spirit, fill those places that are now clean with your love, peace, kindness, gentleness, goodness, self-control, faithfulness, patience, and joy. Praise God. Thank you, Lord.

In the precious name of Jesus I pray,
AMEN

# CONTROL

Father God, I ask that you forgive me for anything I have said, done, thought, watched or listened to that was not of you. I put my trust in you and I lean not on my own understanding. I ask that you would deliver me from my controlling behavior.

*"Trust in the LORD with all thine heart; and lean not unto thine own understanding." Proverbs 3:5*

Today Lord, I bind the spirit of control which I exercise over my *(name: children, spouse, friends, family ect.)* in the name of Jesus. I loose it from my life. I loose humility and the peace of God to rule and reign in my heart and mind. Father, remove the spirit of appeasement, denial, domineering, enabling, false responsibility, female control, jealousy, manipulation, male aggression, passivity, possessiveness, pride and witchcraft. In the name of Jesus, Father, these demonic spirits have opened the door to: *(fear, infirmities, sexual sins, unbelief, rebellion, trauma, mocking, addictions, dependencies, escape, anger, bitterness, violence, depression, shame, unworthiness, failure, abandonment, rejection, broken finances, religion, performance, anxiety, deception, mental problems, and ungodly family patterns).* I close each and every door that has been open for Satan to enter to steal, kill and destroy.

Father, I ask you to fill me with your Holy Spirit and heal me of childhood hurt. I submit my life to you Holy Spirit. Help me to grow and mature in your word that I may work out my soul salvation and learn to exercise self control, resist fleshly desires, and walk in righteousness. Your will be done and your kingdom come in my life today.

I want to be a testimony of your grace, love and mercy.

In the precious name of Jesus I pray,

AMEN

# DEPRESSION

My Father, forgive me for allowing the spirit of depression to take over my heart, mind, body and soul. I understand that opening the door to this spirit causes feelings like: *(abandonment, rejection, anxiety, deception, confusion, forgetfulness, insanity, mind blocks, paranoia, mind racing, schizophrenia, senility, faithlessness, daydreaming, hopelessness, isolation, laziness, procrastination, and excessive sleeping.)* Satan, Jesus rebukes feelings, thoughts and attitudes like: *(withdrawal, apprehension, doubtfulness, fear of being wrong, mistrust, skepticism, suspicion, uncertainty, irresponsibility, defeat, inadequacy, inferiority, insecurity, self-accusing, self-condemning, self-hate, self-punishment, appeasement, betrayed, entrapped, passive, self-pity, suspicious, and unfaithfulness.)* Father, send your warring angels to break down the walls form from words like "bad boy" or "bad girl" and remove all condemnation, defilement, indifference, disgrace, embarrassment, guilt, hate, inferiority and occult involvements.

I bind up every demonic spirit that has tried to come against me in the name of Jesus. Lord, remove all feuding, frustration, hatred, hostility, rage, resentment, retaliation, revenge, spoiled little boy, spoiled little girl, temper tantrums, resistance, stubbornness, self-will, self-suffering, disobedience, contempt, deception, independence, insubordination, and undermining that has led me to: *(cocaine, cigarettes, alcohol, downers, uppers, marijuana, nonprescription drugs, street drugs, tranquilizers, alcohol, caffeine, chocolate, food, computers, gambling, internet, pornography, overspending, sex, sports, television, video games, and demonic music.)* Give me beauty for these ashes, Lord. Give me the oil of joy for mourning and a garment of praise, Jesus.

*"To appoint unto them that mourn in Zion, to give unto them beauty for ashes, the oil of joy for mourning, the garment of praise for the spirit of heaviness." Isaiah 61:3*

I call on the power of your Holy Spirit to send a river of rushing water to cleanse me and quench my thirst. Replace every demonic spirit with the fruit of your spirit and your Beatitudes.

In the name of Jesus,

AMEN

# DECEPTION

Lord Jesus, I ask that you forgive me for being disobedient by breaking your laws. Please remove the spirit of deception from my heart. This spirit has coerced me into lying, secretiveness, deception, blindness, cheating, stealing, confusion, denial, fraudulence, infidelity, treachery, and untrustworthiness towards my *(name persons: children, spouse, friend, boyfriend, girlfriend, mother, father, teacher, boss, etc.)*. I confess and repent of the sin of lying and deception.

Lord, I know that deception has resulted in: *(abandonment, ill-gotten gain, jail time, false religion, anxiety, mental problems, infirmities, control, fear, sexual sins, occult practices, idolatry, opened doors to the demonic, participation in secret societies, cult practices, mind control organization, and demonic rituals.)* I pray with the power and authority given to me by Jesus Christ that each and every demonic spirit will be cast out of my heart, mind, body and soul.

> *"Wherefore putting away lying, speak every man truth with his neighbour: for we are members one of another."*
> *Ephesians 4:25*

I put away lying and deception. I will speak truth and not lies. Lead me, Heavenly Father, not into temptation but deliver me from evil. Lord, replace each evil spirit with the fruit of your Spirit so that I can be more like you. Lord, I put on the full armor to protect my mind, heart, body and soul from every wicked scheme of the devil. I am healed, I am delivered and I have been set free.

In the name of Jesus,
AMEN

# DRUG DEALER 1ST PRAYER

Father God, I dedicate my life to you today. Jesus, I ask that you forgive me of my sins. I believe that you are the son of God. I come seeking you to fill the empty place in my heart; I know that only you can fill it. Please come into my life as my Lord and Savior. Amen.

I have said things and done things that have harmed and destroyed many peoples' lives and today I turn my entire life over to you. I ask you to forgive me for selling drugs, weed, cocaine, speed etc. to people. I ask you to forgive me for destroying families, marriages, men, women, boys and girls by aiding Satan's plan to kill, steal, and destroy this world. Please forgive me for my destructive behavior, selfish desires and love of money.

Merciful Father, I choose to forgive everyone whom I feel is responsible for my behavior – *(name person: my mother, father, sister, brother, grandfather, uncle, aunt or friend)*. I forgive them they didn't know what they were doing or how it would affect my life. Father, I forgive the people who harmed me with rape, incest, molestation, physical abuse or verbal abuse in my childhood, youth, or adult life.

> *"Then said Jesus, Father, forgive them; for they know not what they do." Luke 23:34*

If I was conceived in adultery, fornication, drunkenness, rejection, or rape, I rebuke each and every spirit that came into my life because of that sin and cast it into the lake of burning sulfur in the name of Jesus. Every demonic entrance that was opened through watching sexual or violent television shows and movies, or reading sexual or violent books, or listening to perverted music, I ask that you would bind and cast them away from my eyes and ears. I ask that you would remove any sexual thoughts, patterns, and desires for men, women, animals, children, mother, father, sister, or brother, in the name of Jesus. Today I receive your forgiveness. I choose to stop judging and condemning myself; and I receive your healing and deliverance. Fill me with your pure love. God I ask that you break every demonic assignment against my life and give me your angelic protection. Fill me with the power of your Holy Spirit.

In the name of Jesus,

AMEN

# DRUG DEALER 2ND PRAYER

Lord Jesus, I confess that I have been a drug dealer but today I want to be delivered from that evil path. God, please cleanse my heart and mind and body and soul. I confess and turn away from being a murderer, thief, cheat, and liar. Forgive me for being dishonest, greedy, deceptive, idolatrous, envious, covetous and irresponsible. Cleanse me from jealousy, people pleasing, possessiveness, rivalry, striving, fraudulence, infidelity, secretiveness, selfishness, treachery, trickery, forgetfulness, insanity, mind binding, mind blocking, paranoia, bipolar, rejection, abandonment, and unforgiveness in the name of Jesus.

Father, I have worshiped idols *(such as: my appearance, beauty, children, clothes, food, occupation, position, possession, power, social status, sports, spouse, money, cars, games, jewelry, TV, furniture, paintings, women, men, boyfriends, girlfriends, shoes, self, homes, wealth, piercings, tattoos, pets, boats, motorcycles, people, family, friends)*. I ask that you forgive me.

Lord Jesus, I rebuke and bind every evil spirit that was brought upon me through *(family patterns, family involvements, abuse, addiction, sibling rivalry, fights, feuding, broken marriages, divorces, pride, arrogance, secret societies, cults, false religion, mind control organizations, chronic illness, sickness, lack of affection, lack of attention, fatherless home, poor role models, rejection, drug dealers, parents on drugs, pride, sexual sins, slave mentality, Jezebel syndrome, cutting tongue, tribalism syndrome, fear, anger, idolatry, witchcraft, drugs, alcohol, or worshipping people)* in the name of Jesus.

Father God, I confess sexual immorality *(with: men, women, animals)*. I ask that you would heal each and every piece of my soul which has been affected by joining myself in these sinful relationships. Make my soul whole. I break those soul ties. I have hurt many men/

women by breaking your laws and I pray that you forgive me. Lord, throw every ungodly soul tie I have acquired through my sins and transference and break off evil spirits, diseases and consequences transmitted through illicit sex *(like: HIV, Chlamydia, gonorrhea, herpes, syphilis, warts, unwanted pregnancies, and abortions).*

I forgive each person I have been involved with (names) and I take responsibility for any children who were born out of my sinful actions.

Lord, I need you to rescue, liberate, redeem, heal, and deliver me. I turn my life completely over to you. Lord, clothe me with the belt of truth, the sword of Spirit, the helmet of salvation, the breastplate of righteousness, the shield of faith, and the gospel of peace. I put on the full armor of God so that I can withstand the wicked schemes of the enemy.

Lord, help me to walk in the fruit of the Spirit – love, joy, self-control, peace, patience, kindness gentleness, faithfulness and goodness in the name of Jesus. Heavenly Father, I cover myself with the blood of Jesus Christ and claim his protection over my family, finances, my home, my spirit, my soul and my body. I surrender it all to you today.

I bind the spirit of retaliation from myself and my children and loose it. I loose the peace of God around and about us. Help me to seek you daily so that I and my family can better serve you. Holy Spirit I ask that the Spirit of Christ may dwell in my heart and mind and that I would experience the love of God.

*"And thine ears shall hear a word behind thee, saying, This is the way, walk ye in it, when ye turn to the right hand, and when ye turn to the left." Isaiah 30:21*

Open my eyes, heart, and mind to overflow with your Holy Spirit that is living inside of me. Give me wisdom, knowledge, revelation, understanding and discernment as I read your Word and pray. Direct me to a church where I can grow and establish a better relationship with you.

In the name of Jesus,

AMEN

# ESCAPE

Lord, please help me! I have found a way to escape from life that is not of you. I ask you to forgive me for wanting to give up and throw in the towel. I confess running to drugs, illicit sex, television, movies, alcohol, sleep, relationships, busyness, spending, and suicide attempts instead of running to you.

> *"There hath no temptation taken you but such as is common to man: but God is faithful, who will not suffer you to be tempted above that ye are able; but will with the temptation also make a way to escape, that ye may be able to bear it." 1 Corinthians 10:13*

Father, please bind up the spirit of unbelief, addiction, dependency, laziness, pride, rebellion, anger, bitterness, violence, failure, abandonment, rejection, envy, false religion, performance, anxiety, deception, mental problems, family patterns, infirmities, control, fears, occult, family involvements in the name of Jesus. Forgive me for allowing (names) my children, family members, people in the church, friends, teachers, strangers, bosses, false prophets etc. to affect me more than you. Lord, I ask that you would remove the pain I have felt from (*the church, pastors, first ladies, leaders, presidents, the nation, the war, destruction, corruption in our government, the homeless, starving children, people dying of aids in Africa and US, children being raped, molested and abused, dying starving babies and children, people dying and going to hell, and feeling lonely*) that has caused me to want to escape from (*name things like: my life, family, responsibilities, this world, and reality*). Father, I surrender every person, problem, and situation has caused me to not do your will.

Lord, take this cup of bitterness from me and fill me with your Holy Spirit in the name of Jesus. Send down your love for my loneliness, your courage for my fears, your power for my weakness, your peace for my worry, your strength for my tiredness, your full armor for my protection, your garment of praise for worship, and your help to face each new day.

In the name of Jesus I pray,

AMEN

# FAILURE

Our Father in heaven, I come to you admitting that I have failed you, myself, my children, my family, my friends, my church, my ministry, my finances, my future, my destiny, my dreams, my marriage and my business by making decisions without consulting you first.

*"I [Jesus] can of mine own self do nothing: as I hear, I judge: and my judgment is just; because I seek not mine own will, but the will of the Father which hath sent me."*
*John 5:30*

Help me, Lord, to not seek to do my own will but to do your will. My quick and hasty decisions have caused failure. I have made wrong decisions in my life from the pressure to succeed and win people's approval and acceptance and to avoid rejection. My failed decisions have brought shame, unworthiness, rebellion, bitterness, violence, depression, grief, trauma, anger, unbelief, escape, irresponsibility, addiction, dependencies, family patterns, dishonesty, broken promises, fights, feuds, abandonment, rejection, poor finances, pressure, anxiety, deception, mental problems, occult, fears, sexual sins, infirmities, and open doors for the enemy.

By the power given to me by your son Jesus Christ, I bind every evil spirit that has entered in my life through my failures and cast them out in the name of Jesus. I loose the purpose and plan of God in my life.

Forgive me, Lord, for blaming *(name: my mother, father, spouse, children, friends, family, church, boss, government, nation etc.)* for my failure. I forgive them and I ask that you would soften the hearts of those I have failed that they would forgive me too in the name of Jesus.

Help me, Lord, to get back up again by the leading and the guiding of your Holy Spirit. Lord, remind me to come to you before I make any decisions in my life. Father, align my will with your will so that you may get the glory out of my life, finances, children, friends, church, ministry, businesses, career, education, marriage, and future. Put my life in order, Lord, so I love like you, live like you, think like you, pray like you, and give like you. I know that I am not all I can be but I thank you for not being what I used to be. Fill my heart full of compassion, kindness, and faith strong enough to move mountains.

In the name of Jesus I pray,

AMEN

# FAMILY CURSES

Lord God, forgive my sins, my father's sins and his father's sins. Forgive my mother's sin and her mother's sins. I ask that you forgive the sins of my ancestors (whether African Americans, Native Americans, Asians, or Europeans) for their participation in cultural rituals and traditions that have opened the doors for demonic spirits to enter into my family line.

I bind, renounce and cast out the spirits attached to my involvement or my family's involvement in *(name: curses, spells, hexes, voodoo, Wicca, and witchcraft)* and false religions and cults *(name: Jehovah's witnesses, New Age Movement, Unitarian churches, The Way International, Scientology and Rastafarianism)* and Secret Societies *(name: Eastern Star Lodge, Elks Lodge, Free Masonry, college fraternities and sororities)*.

Father God, sever all sins and the resulting curses that have been handed down to me by my ancestors. I break their power from my life, and from the life of my descendants in the name of Jesus and by the power of his blood.

In the name of Jesus,
AMEN

# FAMILY INVOLVEMENTS

Heavenly Father, I come interceding on behalf of my family who have omitted or discounted or twisted the foundations of the Christian faith, (i.e. the Trinity, the atonement, the blood of Jesus or divinity of Jesus) through their involvement in *(name: secret societies, cults, false religions, the occult, mind control organizations, Armstrongism, Baha'i, Buddhism, Buffalos, Christadelphians, Christian Science, college fraternities and sororities, Daughters of the Nile, De Malay Lodge, Druids Lodge, Eastern Religions, Eastern Star Lodge, Edgar Cayce, Elks Lodge, Free Masonry, Hare Krishna, Hinduism, Indian Occult Rituals, African Occult Rituals, Rastafarianism, Inner Peace Movement, Islamic Religions, Jehovah Witnesses, Jobs Daughters Lodge, Kabala, KKK, Knights of Columbus Lodge, Masonic, Moonies, Moose Lodge, Mormonism, New Age Movement, Odd Fellows Lodge, Orange Lodge, Rainbow Lodge, Religious Science, Santeria, Satanism, Scientology, Shamanism, Shintoism, Shiners, Silva Mind Control, Spiritualism, Knights Templars, The Way International or The Christian Educational Society, Theosophy, Unitarian Church, Voodoo, Wicca, White Shrine, witchcraft, sin of Balaam, Kabala, Astrology, or Diviners.)* These names are all under the power and authority given to me by Jesus Christ, his power is greater than any other power.

I break all chords, ties, chains, and strongholds twenty five generations back on both my mother's and father's side, in the name of Jesus. Lord God, I ask that you would break all demonic ties, rebuke all spirits, and family patterns *(such as: unbelief, mockery, addictions, dependencies, escape, apathy, indifference, pride, rebellion, anger, bitterness, violence, depression, trauma, grief, shame, unworthiness, failure, abandonment, rejection, financial struggles, performance, anxiety, deception, mental problems, infirmities, disease, control, fears, and sexual sins)* that have been active in my life or my parents and ancestors.

Lord, bring my family love, connection, peace, strength, and salvation. Help us, Lord, to walk in your ways.

In the name of Jesus I pray,

AMEN

# FAMILY PATTERNS

Heavenly Father, please forgive my sinful behavior which transferred to my family, friends, and strangers through my bloodline, associations, soul ties, lying on of hands, psychic prayers, witchcraft, curses and physical contact. Lord, I bind these powers in the air right now! I break every demonic assignment.

> *"Verily I say unto you, Whatsoever ye shall bind on earth shall be bound in heaven: and whatsoever ye shall loose on earth shall be loosed in heaven." Matthew 18:18*

I ask for the power and anointing of the Holy Spirit to administer the gifts of the Spirit necessary for breaking down every family pattern, curse, and stronghold. I ask for your angelic intervention to overthrow my family's patterns of abusive or poor communication, lack of intimacy or faithfulness in marriage, the domination of men over women or women over men, deceptive business practices, financial losses, family secrets, broken promises, unfilled lives and destinies, divorce, addictions, suicide, abuse, rape, and molestation.

Lord send forth your angels to battle demonic assignments against the children in my family through favoritism, neglect, lack of affection and attention, sibling rivalry, fights, feuds, divorce, fatherless home dishonoring parents, pride, poor role models, possessions, clothes, appearance, social status, slave mentality, bitterness, insecurity, depression, chronic illness, sickness, cancer, diabetes, heart disease, premature deaths, fear, anger, witchcraft, and drugs. Satan, the Lord Jesus Christ rebukes you.

Heavenly Father, destroy the bondages caused through the occult, false religions, cults, secret societies and gangs. I declare Jesus Christ is far above all rule and authority. In the name of Jesus, I break every stronghold, curse, and chain binding my family twenty-five generations down on mother's side and father's side.

In the name of Jesus it shall be done,
AMEN

# FEARS

Lord, you have not given me the spirit of fear, but the spirit of love, peace, and sound mind.

*"For God hath not given us the spirit of fear; but of power, and of love, and of a sound mind." 2 Timothy 1:7*

So today, I confess my fear as not coming from you. I ask that you forgive me for my anxiety, bewilderment, burden, dread, harassment, heaviness, horror, intimidation, mental torment, over sensitivity, paranoia, phobia, superstitions, worry, fear of being attacked, fear of being wrong, fear of being a victim, fear of cancer, fear of diabetes, fear of demons, fear of exposure, fear of failure, fear of having a heart attack, fear of inadequacy, fear of infirmities, fear of loss, fear of men, fear of women, fear of performing, fear of poverty, fear of public singing, fear of public praying, fear of preaching, fear of teaching, fear of punishment, fear of rejection, fear of sexual inadequacy, fear of success, fear of violence, fear of being raped, fear of being used, fear of being hurt, fear of being alone, fear of being loved, fear of loving someone, fear of being married, fear of being dumped, and fear of all diseases.

Lord, I rebuke every fearful spirit and ask that you replace them with love, joy, peace, patience, self-control, goodness, gentleness, faithfulness, and kindness. I surrender my thoughts, mind, heart, body and soul to you.

In the name of Jesus I pray,
AMEN

# FORGIVENESS

Father, I come to you today asking that you forgive me for the spirit of unforgiveness. Lord, my unforgiveness has hardened my heart and I ask that you would soften my heart. Lord, my heart has been kicked, stepped on, beat up, crushed and now it is bleeding. Lord, please take away all the hurt and pain of unforgiveness and heal me.

Lord, I choose to forgive *(name: my mother, father, grandfather, grandmother; brother, sister, aunts, cousins, uncle, pastor, friends, church family, enemies)* so that you can heal and deliver me as well as heal and deliver each person I named. I forgive them for abusing me: spiritually, mentally, verbally, and physically. I forgive them for raping me, molesting me, blocking me from my blessing, blocking me from ministry, rejecting me, trying to kill, steal, and destroy me, slandering me, hindering me from praying, singing and preaching. Satan, Jesus rebukes you.

I need your help, Lord, to love others as you have loved me – unconditionally. I need your love that is patient, kind, does not envy, does not boast, is not proud, is not rude, is not self-seeking, is not easily angered, keeps no record of wrong, does not delight in evil but rejoices with the truth, always protects, always trust, always hopes, and never fails. Lord, please give me your love that seeks the highest good of others.

Give me joy and gladness not based on circumstances. Give me your peace, contentment, patience and unity with others. Make me slow to speak and slow to anger. Make me kind, merciful, sweet and tender. Make me generous, openhearted, faithful, dependable, loyal, trustworthy, gentle, humble, calm, non-threatening, self-controlled, and well-behaved. In the name of Jesus equip me with your full armor – the belt of God's truth to remove lies, the breastplate of righteousness to protect my heart, the footgear of peace to spread the good news. Equip me with the shield of faith to protect me from the flaming arrows of the enemy, the helmet of salvation to protect my mind and give me eternal life, and the sword of the spirit to destroy the works of the enemy.

Victory is mine in the name of Jesus,

AMEN

# GRIEF PRAYER ONE

My Father in heaven, I come weary, broken and heavy laden, knowing that you can ease my grief. Lord, the death of my (name: mother, father, brother, friend etc.) has brought me to a state of mourning. Lord, I know that mourning is healthy but excessive mourning has built a barrier to my relationship with you.

> *"But the Comforter, which is the Holy Ghost, whom the Father will send in my name, he shall teach you all things, and bring all things to your remembrance, whatsoever I have said unto you." John 14:26*

Lord, please forgive me for any ways that I have reacted to grief that is not of you *(like: violence, rebellion, shame, apathy, escape, isolation, addictions, unbelief, bitterness, control, occult practices, fear, sexual sins, and deception).*

I give you the financial burdens, weakness, loss, physical and mental problems, relationships in my life that have left me crying and feeling agony, anguish, despair, heartbreak, pain, sadness, sorrow, torment, and weeping. In the name of Jesus I rebuke every ungodly emotion Lord and ask that you take complete control over my emotions and mind. I receive your comfort, peace, happiness, joy, strength, power and sound mind.

In the name of Jesus I pray,
AMEN

# GRIEF PRAYER TWO

Father God, I come asking that you would forgive me for grief that hinders my relationship with you. Break the stronghold of grief in my life from loss whether it was the loss of *(name: person, marriage, job, work, baby or child, relationships, transportation, home, investment, business or sentimental possessions)*. Lord, please forgive me if I have trusted in myself or have idolized anything that I mentioned.

> *"But we had the sentence of death in ourselves, that we should not trust in ourselves, but in God which raiseth the dead." 2 Corinthians 1:9*

Lord, I thank you for saving me from hopelessness and releasing hope back into my life. Thank you for never leaving me even when I abandoned you and your will. I ask that you restore my life, my mind, my emotions, my thoughts, my speech, my character, my appetite, and my body in the name of Jesus.

Clothe me with the full armor of God, the armor of light, the armor of righteousness.

In the name of Jesus,

AMEN

# HOMOSEXUALITY (LESBIAN, GAY, BISEXUAL)

Spirit of the living God, I ask that you would forgive me for living an ungodly lifestyle by submitting to a homosexual spirit and walking in unrighteousness *(as a lesbian, homosexual, "down low" brother or "down low" woman, bisexual, rapist, molester, or abuser)* Lord God, I choose to forgive the one (name) who raped and molested me, the one (name) who beat me, the one (name) who physically abused me, the one (name) who verbally abused me, and the one (name) who caused me any kind of pain.

Lord, I ask for your forgiveness for allowing these past hurts and pain to affect my conscious, subconscious, and unconscious mind. I repent of all my sins. I renounce the sin of my forefathers. I break free from all the demonic designs on my life. I break free from all hereditary curses through conception, childhood, transference, a perverse spirit, rejection, fornication, adultery, drunkenness, incest, bestiality, bloodlines, soul ties, the laying on hands, psychic prayers, and witchcraft twenty-five generations down through my parents.

During my sexual sins a piece of my soul was deposited in each person. Today I call back every broken piece of my soul that was deposited in each and every person named. Lord, deliver me from every evil work, Lord, guide me in all my relationships. Heavenly Father, I believe that you have forgiven me. I accept your forgiveness, and I no longer judge and condemn myself.

Lord, preserve and keep me pure and holy. Lord, help me to keep marriage between a woman and a man sacred. Lord, help me to remember that my body is a temple of the Holy Spirit and you live inside of me. Lord I surrender my physical appetites to Christ's lordship and my sexuality for the glory of God.

In the name of Jesus I pray,
AMEN

# INFIRMITIES AND
# DISEASE 1ST PRAYER

Father God, I come binding the powers of darkness and loosing the power of righteousness by the Holy Ghost. I break every assignment from the powers in the air. I ask for angelic protection and the gift of healing needed to minister this prayer. In the name of Jesus, I loose confusion into the camp of the enemy. I bind up the spirit of (name the disease). I bind up the spirit of destruction, witchcraft, death, secret sins and sickness in the name of Jesus.

Every door that was opened for the demonic to enter because of sins *(like: alcohol, drugs, sexual sin, occult involvement, cultic and occult readings, pornographic movies or literature, iniquities of the mother and father, cursed womb, rape, incest, abuse, addictions, blood line curses, mind control, hypnosis, and mediation)* I shut those doors. I bind and cast out these demonic strongholds. Any open doors because of tragedies, accidents, trauma, guilt, shame, condemnation, death of loved ones, fear, depression, and ungodly soul ties I close in the name of Jesus.

Bitterness, insecurity, rebellion, jealousy, pride, strife, lust, control, worry, guilt, passivity, indecision, cursing, gluttony, grief and carnality must leave. With the authority given to me by Jesus Christ, who is far above all rule and authority, I cast you out.

Lord, fill these cleaned out areas with the fruit of your Spirit – love, peace, joy, patience, kindness, goodness, gentleness, faithfulness and self-control. Heavenly Father, give me knowledge, wisdom, and understanding into your life. Equip me with the full armor of God – the helmet of salvation, breastplate of righteousness, shield of faith, belt of truth, foot gear of readiness to spread the good news, and the sword of the spirit, so that I may withstand the wicked schemes of the enemy.

I surrender my life to you as a living sacrifice. I declare that by the stripes of Jesus I am healed. You have sent your word to heal me. Lord, I receive my healing. Pain, discomfort and infirmity must go. I choose to walk in my healing and my deliverance. I put my faith in you, Lord, for my healing.

In the name of Jesus,

AMEN

(Inspired by Freeman)

# INFIRMITIES AND DISEASE
# 2ND PRAYER

In the name of Jesus Christ, I bind the powers of darkness attacking my body and break every demonic assignment against me. I loose peace. Peace from the demonic assignment. Peace of God come. I ask for your angelic protection, Jesus. By faith I ask for gifts of the spirit needed to minister this prayer. I cast out the infirmities of *(name the infirmity: arthritis, anorexia, bulimia, asthma, bareness, cancer, congestion, diabetes, the heart, the lungs, mental illness, MS, migraines, the brain, cataract, deafness, or AIDs).* Satan, Jesus rebukes you and every infirmity that has opened the door to receive *(name: a pace maker, fatigue, female problems, circulatory problems, physical abnormalities, premature death, mental problems, or emotional problems).*

I close the doors to demonic attacks which have affected my *(name: blood, bones, muscles, eyes, ears, speech, sexual character, appetite, nervous system, respiratory system, endocrine and digestive systems).*

I bind up those infirmities and close every open door by the authority given to me in Jesus Christ who is far above all rule and authority. I loose the peace of God to rule and reign in my heart, mind and soul.

> *"Who his own self bare our sins in his own body on the tree,*
> *that we, being dead to sins, should live unto righteousness:*
> *by whose stripes ye were healed." 1 Peter 2:24*

I am healed by Jesus' stripes. I will walk in wholeness, health and healing.

In the name of Jesus,
AMEN

# IDOLATRY

Lord, I come asking that you forgive me for the sin of idolatry. I have put my appearance, beauty, children, clothes, food, ministry, occupation, position, possessions, power, social status, sports, or wealth before you. I repent. God, I ask that you would forgive me.

> *"I am the LORD, and there is none else, there is no God beside me." Isaiah 45:5*

In the name of Jesus I break all soul ties, strongholds, chains, chords, and bondages. Lord, forgive me. You are my God. You are my life. I can live without eating meat, shopping, getting my hair and nails done, cars, boats, jewelry, boyfriend or girlfriend, a certain job, famous brand clothing and shoes, a spouse, money, or parents. Pursuing these things has caused me to break the first and second commandment. Lord, remove any and every idol which is hindering my personal relationship with you. Lord God, I can live without possession, position, relationships but I can't live without you. Strengthen my faith. Help me to trust and remove anything or anybody that would entice, persuade, or encourage me to break you laws.

In the name of Jesus I pray, AMEN

# MOCKING

Lovely Heavenly Father, I close every door to demonic spirits which have spoken against you (like television, radio, books, comics, computers, magazines, friends, or family). I command these mocking demonic spirits to be silenced and unable to speak blaspheme, sarcasm, curses, and profanity, or to ridicule, laugh at, or scorn the name of Jesus.

*"Set a watch, O LORD, before my mouth; keep the door of my lips." Psalm 141:3*

Lord, set a watch over my mouth and purify my lips as with a coal, so I speak truth in love.

*"Then said I, Woe is me! for I am undone; because I am a man of unclean lips, and I dwell in the midst of a people of unclean lips: for mine eyes have seen the King, the LORD of hosts. Then flew one of the seraphims unto me, having a live coal in his hand, which he had taken with the tongs from off the altar: And he laid it upon my mouth, and said, Lo, this hath touched thy lips; and thine iniquity is taken away, and thy sin purged." Isaiah 6:5-7*

I put on the belt of truth so that every word I speak is done in love by the leading of the Holy Spirit.

When I am tempted to say defiled things, help me to speak things that will build and uplift my brothers and sisters.

Lord train me to speak words that bring life. Help me to speak life and not death. According to Psalms chapter 19 verse 14, Let the words of my mouth and the meditation of my heart be acceptable in your sight, O Lord my strength and my redeemer.

In the name of Jesus,
AMEN

# MOLESTATION OR MOLESTER

Lord Jesus, I ask that you would intercede for me according to God's will through this prayer.

> *"Wherefore he [Jesus] is able also to save them to the uttermost that come unto God by him, seeing he ever liveth to make intercession for them." Hebrews 7:25*

Holy Spirit, I ask that you cover me with the blood of Jesus Christ. I come asking you to forgive me for my sinful acts, thoughts and deeds. I bind the spirit of molestation which came in through the actions of *(name person: friend, cousin, uncle, brother, sister, mother, father, uncle, aunt, mother's boyfriend, father's girlfriend, stepmother, stepfather, foster parents, grandmother, grandfather, pastor, preacher, teacher, or neighbor)* in the name of Jesus. Satan, I bind you and loose you from transferring this spirit through bloodlines, soul ties, association, curses, childhood incidents, or family patterns in the name of Jesus. Holy Spirit, restore and heal me from molestation, the aftermath of traumatization, victimization, mental torment, depression, fear, denial, infirmities, violence, shame, anger, bitterness, low self-esteem, suicidal thoughts and actions, confusion, rejection, insanity, and forgetfulness. Paranoia, schizophrenia, hate, sex change, drug addiction, alcoholism, gambling, gluttony, pornography, stripping, sexual activity, promiscuousness, fornication, adultery, jealousy, insecurity, strife, lust, control, worry, guilt, passivity, indecision, abandonment, cursing, grief, murder, abortions, carnality, occultism, embarrassment, unbelief, and unforgiveness you must leave. I bind up and cast out the demonic spirit of molestation from me and my family line back twenty-five generations.

I call back the shattered pieces of my soul that were broken during the act of molestation. Holy Spirit, make me whole, give me a new beginning and use me to glorify your name. Teach me how to love and forgive the person (names) who molested me. God, I bless the person who molested me. I ask that you break this cycle of pain and sin. Fill me with your Spirit and the fruits of the spirit. I put on the full armor of God. Holy Spirit, use my life to bless others. In the name of Jesus, AMEN

# OCCULT

Lord, I have broken you commandments. I have practiced idolatry and witchcraft through fortune telling, automatic handwriting, mental telepathy, horoscopes, hypnosis, astral projection, psychic reading, past life, palm reading, pendulum reading, psychic healing, hexing, voodoo, water witching, Ouija Board, spirit guides, séances, Eastern meditation, table tipping, tarot cards, ESP, astrology and tea leaves reading. Heavenly Father, I confess and repent for these sins.

> *"Behold, to obey is better than sacrifice, and to hearken than the fat of rams. For rebellion is as the sin of witchcraft, and stubbornness is as iniquity and idolatry." 1 Samuel 15:22-23*

By breaking your commandments, Lord, I have opened up demonic doors to curses, the Jezebel spirit, confusion, deception, being accident prone, spirits of suicide, and false gifts. Satan, I bind you. In the name of Jesus, I break every demonic spell that has been cast on my life and family back twenty-five generations. Victory is mine. In Christ I am more than a conqueror.

> *"In all these things we are more than conquerors through him that loved us. For I am persuaded, that neither death, nor life, nor angels, nor principalities, nor powers, nor things present, nor things to come, Nor height, nor depth, nor any other creature, shall be able to separate us from the love of God, which is in Christ Jesus our Lord." Romans 8:37-39*

I rebuke and cast out every evil spirit that has entered by body or my mind. In the name of Jesus I break every demonic chain, cord, and stronghold that has tried to ruin my life. I break every curse spoken against me, my children, family, church, or ministry twenty-five generation down on my mother's side and my father's side in the name of Jesus. Send your angelic protection. Cover me with your wings of protection, Lord Jesus. Send your grace and your anointing, Lord Jesus, so that your will may be done in my life. I can rest in your love and peace.

In the precious name of Jesus I pray,
AMEN

# PERFORMANCE

Lord, please forgive me for trying to perform for acceptance and gain. I have damaged my health, relationships, past, present, and future. I have not trusted you and your will for my life.

> *"Except the LORD build the house, they labour in vain that build it: except the LORD keep the city, the watchman waketh but in vain. It is vain for you to rise up early, to sit up late, to eat the bread of sorrows: for so he giveth his beloved sleep." Psalm 127:1-2*

Performance has opened the door to evil spirits like competition, being driven, envy, jealousy, people pleasing, perfectionism, possessiveness, rivalry, striving and workaholism. Lord God, in the name of Jesus I ask that you would remove every evil spirit and replace them with love, joy, self-control, patience, peace, faithfulness, goodness, and gentleness.

Heavenly Father, I ask that you would bless me with supernatural mountain-moving faith. Give me the confirmation to know that I am walking in your will and what you have for me. No devil in hell can take that from me. I love you, Lord, because you have heard my cry and I stand on your word that the best is yet to come.

In the name of Jesus,
AMEN

# POVERTY

Heavenly Father, for so long – generation after generation – my family has allowed the spirit of poverty to encircle our lives. Psalm 30:8 says, *Give me neither poverty nor riches but feed me with food that I need for today.*

Today I bind the spirit of poverty off my life and family twenty-five generations down in the name of Jesus. I rebuke all spoken curses of poverty off of my life and my children's life. I ask that you, Lord Jesus, make me spiritually rich in my soul as you continue to give me my daily bread.

Keep me from the love of money which is the root of all evil. I ask that you would bless me and my family with financial provision and help us to become good stewards over your money. Help me to earn honestly, spend wisely, give generously and invest carefully, Father.

Help me, lead me, and guide me in using my wealth to fund your kingdom and tear the devil's kingdom. I speak spiritual prosperity, financial prosperity, physical prosperity, and mental prosperity into my life in the name of Jesus. Lord, you are everything to me so I ask that you will be my investor, banker, financial advisor, bank, lawyer, provider, stronghold, strong tower, strength, redeemer, daily bread, healer, deliverer, shelter, advocate, restorer, hiding place, resting place, refuge from the storm, peace, shield, wonderful counselor, hope, and comfort.

I pray that the Spirit of the Lord will lift up my head as I walk in prosperity for the rest of my life.

In the name of Jesus,
AMEN

# PRIDE

Lord God, I come surrendering my attitude and ask that you would forgive me for having a prideful spirit. Lord, I rebuke this prideful spirit and every spirit that has attached itself to me like – conceit, control, self-focus, haughtiness, leviathan, prejudice, self-centeredness, self-importance, insanity, self-rule, self-reliance, dominance, sins of omission, sins of commission, sins of speech, and arrogance in the name of Jesus.

*"Let nothing be done through strife or vainglory; but in lowliness of mind let each esteem other better than themselves." Philippians 2:3*

Father, I call on the anointing of your Holy Spirit to overcome, bind, rebuke and cast out the devil when these spirits try to arise in my life, behavior or attitudes.

I need your grace and your mercy to keep me humble so that I may be a light in the darkness. Instead of seeking glory, I want you to receive all of the glory from my life. Lord, help me to esteem others and bless the people you bring into my life in the name of Jesus.

Lord, I say yes to your way, yes to your will and yes to your plan for my life. Lord, I want to be obedient, I want to be holy, I want to be pure and I want to be focused on you.

In the name of Jesus I pray,
AMEN

# RAPE OR RAPIST

Heavenly Father, I humble myself before you. I cover myself in the blood of Jesus Christ. I bind the spirit of rape in the name of Jesus. I loose the love of God. I was hurt by the actions of *(name of person: mother, father, adoptive parents, boy or girlfriend, spouse, cousin, stepfather, brother, uncle, stepmother, sister, aunt, mother's boyfriend, best friend, minister, pastor, bishop, first lady, teacher, mentor or neighbor).* Satan, I rebuke you from transferring this spirit through my bloodline, soul ties, associations, curses, childhood incidents, secrets, domination, or family patterns and cycles in the name of Jesus.

Lord, help me recover and heal from rape aftermath. Heavenly Father, heal me of trauma, feelings of unworthiness, victimization, depression, fear, denial, infirmities, diseases, violence, shame, mocking, anger, bitterness, low self-esteem, suicidal thoughts and actions, confusion, self-hatred, rejection, craziness, and forgetfulness. Satan, Jesus rebukes you – paranoia, schizophrenia, hysteria, hallucinations, insanity, worry, nervousness, people pleasing, self-pity, man hating, women hating, sex change, drug addiction, alcoholism, gambling, cigarettes, gluttony, pornography, stripping, sexually immorality, fornication, and adultery.

Lord, I come with a repentant heart asking that you forgive me. Today I choose to forgive and bless (person's name) who raped me.

> *"And be ye kind one to another, tenderhearted, forgiving one another, even as God for Christ's sake hath forgiven you." Ephesians 4:32*

I call back the shattered pieces of my soul that were broken off during the act of rape in the name of Jesus. I am now complete in

Jesus Christ. Lord, cleanse and wash me with the water of your word. Purify me – spirit, soul and body! In Christ I am holy and blameless by the blood of Jesus. Help me, Father, to respect my body which is your temple by keeping it holy and covering it modestly. Send the spirit of love, peace, joy, patience, kindness, goodness, faithfulness, gentleness and self-control in my life and my attacker's life.

In the name of Jesus,
AMEN

# REBELLION

Lord Jesus, I come confessing my rebellion again you and those in authority *(name: my mother, father, mentors, pastor, leaders, grandmother, grandfather, elders, boss, teachers and police).*

> *"Submitting yourselves one to another in the fear [respect] of God." Ephesians 5:21*

Help me, Lord, to humble myself and show respect and honor to those in authority. I rebuke this rebellious spirit of contempt, defiance, disobedience, independence, insubordination, resistance, self-sufficiency, self-will, stubbornness and disrespect in the name of Jesus. Lord, I bind, break down and cast out all demonic spirits attached to this spirit of rebellion. Lord, I ask you to forgive me. I need your love, your grace, your mercy, and your strength, Lord. I break every rebellious spirit off my children and family line twenty-five generation down in the name of Jesus.

I want to be respectful, submissive and obedient. I want to do right. Lord, heal, redeem and restore me so that your will may be done through me. Let me be a light to my generation, shine through me.

In the name of Jesus I pray, AMEN

# REBELLIOUS SON

Heavenly Father, I come confessing my sins (name them) especially sins of rebellion against you and those in authority. By allowing rebellion in my life, I have opened the door for other demonic spirits to enter like the spirit of anger, disrespectfulness, mocking, bitterness, unbelief, self-pity, performance, deception, cutting tongue, idolatry, witchcraft, cave man mentality, bloody warrior syndrome, slave mentality, co-dependency, depression, resentment, unforgiveness, strife, fighting, conflict, discord, and turmoil. I bind and cast out these spirits of darkness and I loose the light of God, in the name of Jesus.

> *"And the son said unto him, Father, I have sinned against heaven, and in thy sight, and am no more worthy to be called thy son. But the father said to his servants, Bring forth the best robe, and put it on him; and put a ring on his hand, and shoes on his feet: And bring hither the fatted calf, and kill it; and let us eat, and be merry: For this my son was dead, and is alive again; he was lost, and is found. And they began to be merry." Luke 15:21-24*

Lord, I repent for being rebellious. I come back to you. Thank you for receiving me with open arms.

Thank you for the blood of Jesus that removes my sins as far away as the East is from the West. Fill me with your Holy Spirit and the fruits of the Spirit – love, peace, and joy in the Holy Spirit.

In the name of Jesus,
AMEN

# REJECTION

Lord Jesus, I come to you asking for healing and forgiveness. I have been rejected and have rejected. Please forgive me for rejecting you and your instructions for my life. I rebuke, bind and cast out the spirit of rejection which has operated in me and I loose the love of God in this relationship between me and *(name: my mother, father, aunt, uncle, cousins, teacher, pastors, boss, co-worker, friends, and enemies)* in the name of Jesus.

I chose to stop expecting rejection, perceiving rejection, and self-rejecting. Living in rejection has affected my ability to love, to forgive, to grieve, to share, to care, to heal, to give, to marry, to prosper, to please, to be humble, and to behave well. Stop and reverse that cycle, Lord.

> *"Blessed be the God and Father of our Lord Jesus Christ, who hath blessed us with all spiritual blessings in heavenly places in Christ: According as he hath chosen us in him before the foundation of the world, that we should be holy and without blame before him in love: Having predestinated us unto the adoption of children by Jesus Christ to himself, according to the good pleasure of his will, To the praise of the glory of his grace, wherein he hath made us accepted in the beloved." Ephesians 1:3-6*

Heavenly Father, thank you for giving me every spiritual blessing, choosing me, making me holy and blameless, adopting me as your child and accepting me.

Lord, help me to accept and seek your highest good for others. Help me to be a peacemaker, bringing unity between people. May I be quick to hear, slow to speak and slow to anger, merciful, loving and tender, generous and open hearted, dependable, loyal, trustworthy, humble, calm, non-threatening and self-controlled.

In the name of Jesus,
AMEN

# RELIGIOUS SPIRIT

Lord, I ask for your forgiveness for hindering your Holy Spirit by operating with a spirit of judgment, control, legalism, and religiosity. This religious spirit has divided and influenced your church and congregation. I call on the power of your anointing to break down every wall and every evil spirit operating in the church – spirits of the antichrist, betrayal, denominationalism, division, hypocrisy, injustice, legalism, liberalism, New Age practices, religiosity, spiritual pride, traditionalism, and unforgiveness – that have kept the congregation from worshipping you in spirit and in truth.

Lord, free the congregation's heart, mind, body and soul from everything that is not of you –believing man's writings are become more important than scripture itself, thinking that all supernatural highs are from God, operating in soulish realms, being fearful of anything emotional, establishing rituals, methods, practices, and formulas, dictating how the congregation should dress, praise, or confess, building doctrinal walls and elevating church positions and offices – which lead to separation, pride and exclusiveness. These ways must go in the name of Jesus. Lord, I will be an intercessor and pray that you break down and cast out every evil spirit on assignment to kill, steal and destroy my church. Free us so we can love and serve one another, Lord.

> *"For, brethren, ye have been called unto liberty; only use not liberty for an occasion to the flesh, but by love serve one another." Galatians 5:13*

Jesus, remove any leaders, traditions, or rituals that hinder the work of your Holy Spirit. Clean house, Lord, and send us a fresh anointing.

I ask for a double portion of your Spirit to be upon my house, children, family, church, and pastor. I pray for the gifts of the Spirit to operate decently and in order in my life and church. Lord, please help us to walk after the Spirit and start manifesting the fruit of love, joy, peace, patience, kindness, goodness, gentleness, and self-control. In the name of Jesus, AMEN

# SEXUAL SINS

Father God, I confess my sinful and impure thoughts, attitudes, words, relationships, and actions. Lord, these sexual sins – abortion, adultery, bestiality, demonic sex, exposure, seduction, sexual fantasies, lust, fornication, prostitution, homosexuality, rape, incest, sexual abuse, lesbianism, masturbation, pornography have opened the door of my life to demons.

I repent of my sins and ask for your forgiveness, Lord God. Under all power and authority given to me by Jesus, Satan, I command you to flee. Take your hands off of my body, marriage, family, mind, finances, and emotions you must go. I break every curse spoken against me, every cross prayer, every plan of Satan, every hex and every spell in the name of Jesus and by the power of his blood. I expose the deeds of darkness to your light, Heavenly Father.

> *"For ye were sometimes darkness, but now are ye light in the Lord: walk as children of light: (For the fruit of the Spirit is in all goodness and righteousness and truth;) Proving what is acceptable unto the Lord. And have no fellowship with the unfruitful works of darkness, but rather reprove them. For it is a shame even to speak of those things which are done of them in secret. But all things that are reproved are made manifest by the light: for whatsoever doth make manifest is light." Ephesians 5:8-13*

I claim deliverance, healing and wholeness over my life in the name of Jesus. Holy Spirit, place your angelic protection over and around my life. Replace every ungodly spirit with the fruit of the Spirit – goodness, love and self-control. Lord, clothe me with the full armor of God to hold on to my deliverance and freedom. Give me a hunger for reading your word and prayer. Help me walk in the light.

In the precious name of Jesus I pray,
AMEN

# SEXUAL RELATIONS (NOT MARRIED)

Heavenly Father, please forgive me for sexual immorality – adultery and fornication. My sinful actions violate your laws. I have walked after my flesh and been self-focused. I have destroyed families and my testimony. Lord, I repent.

My Father, I break every soul tie with the people I have had sex with (name them). Lord, please put every missing piece from my soul back together and make me whole. Lord, I give you my feelings of hurt, anger, bitterness, violence, depression, shame, grief, trauma, devastation, rebellion, unbelief, unworthiness, fear, failure, abandonment, hopelessness, rejection, anxiety, and deception. Lord, heal me of the negative consequences of my sins – mental problems, sickness, drug addictions, alcoholism, smoking, gambling, isolation, sexually transmitted diseases, apathy, forgetfulness, laziness, procrastination, irresponsibility, escaping into sleep, crying, gluttony, unwanted pregnancies, thoughts of suicide, and lack of trust – these must cease their operation.

*"Casting down imaginations, and every high thing that exalteth itself against the knowledge of God, and bringing into captivity every thought to the obedience of Christ." 2 Corinthians 10:5*

Lord, I ask for a fresh start, a new beginning. Help me to be obedient to your laws, cast down imaginations and take every thought captive that tries to exalt itself above your will. Help me to resist sexual temptation and flee from those places and friends that tempt me to do things that are not according to your word. Help me to diligently guard my mind and not read books or watch movies that stir up the lust of the flesh. Help me to honor sex as a gift to be given only to my spouse in marriage. Help me to be satisfied with my spouse and not look for any affection outside of our marriage. Your word says the love of God has been shed aboard in my heart so I choose to let your love flow through me to my spouse or the one you have set aside for me. Help me to desire the marriage partner you have chosen and to wait on your time table not my own.

I ask these things in the precious name of Jesus,
AMEN

# SHAME

Heavenly Father, for a long time I have hung my head in shame over my sins, situations and disobedience. I have been ashamed of myself, my family, my children, my mother, my husband, my father, my sister, and my brother. I have been ashamed of being poor, my lack of education, my home, my performance, my intelligence, my ethnicity, my community, and my health. I have been ashamed of sexual sins, addictions, having an abortion, having been raped or molested. These shameful things have resulted in being unforgiving, addicted, unbelieving, violent, bitter, secretive, unmotivated, controlling, fearful, sick, mentally disturbed, deceptive, or a people pleaser.

Father God, I confess and repent of being ashamed of and disrespecting my mother, father, grandparents, authority figures, and ancestors *(name: African, Asian, white, Native American)*. Lord, I pray by the power of the Holy Spirit that the spirit of shame would be bound and cast out of my life. I confess being judgmental and condemning of myself, others and even God. Lord, forgive me. I forgive each person who has hurt me and caused shame.

> *"And the LORD shall make thee the head, and not the tail; and thou shalt be above only, and thou shalt not be beneath; if that thou hearken unto the commandments of the LORD thy God, which I command thee this day, to observe and to do them." Deuteronomy 28:13*

Thank you that I can hold my head up high and not bent in shame. Lord, you have made me the head and not the tail, and have placed me above and not beneath. Lord, help me to be obedient and do everything you want me to do, keep my heart right. Put my life in order, prepare me, and plant me where I will bear the fruit of your Spirit. Show me my purpose, keep me in the center of your will, protect me, and give me wisdom, knowledge, understanding, revelation, and discernment. Let me speak words that bring life and change me into the likeness of Christ. Lead me out of my past into my future.

In the name of Jesus I pray,

AMEN

# SUICIDE

Lord Jesus, you sacrificed yourself for me so I could live. You have a special purpose for my life. Today I come asking for your forgiveness for trying to commit suicide. I confess and repent for my destructive thoughts and actions.

By the power and the authority in the name of Jesus and the blood of Jesus, I rebuke, bind and cast out this suicidal spirit from my life. Whether the spirit of suicide and death entered my life because of emotional, physical, mental, sexual, spiritual, or verbal abuse, it must leave now in the name of Jesus.

Lord, I choose to forgive *(person's name: my mother, father, kids at school, sister, brother, pastor, church, uncle, or neighbor)* who hurt and violated me. Forgive me for my sinful reactions – judging, trying to kill myself, seeking vengeance, and hating them. Work in their lives to heal and deliver them.

Lord, remove and cleanse me of anger, fear, bitterness, shame, a victim's mentality, trauma, grief, addictions, violence, depression, lack of motivation, unbelief, rebellion, unworthiness, abandonment, rejection, anxiety, deception, escapism, infirmities, control, fear, and sexual sins in the name of Jesus.

Thank you for giving me life, Jesus, through your death. I choose to live as a child of God. Give me an appreciation for life – all life.

> *"For I know the thoughts that I think toward you, saith the LORD, thoughts of peace, and not of evil, to give you an expected end." Jeremiah 29:11*

Thank you for the plans you have for me to give me a future filled with hope. Fill me with your strength, grace, mercy, wisdom, knowledge, understanding, discernment, love, peace, patience, joy, goodness, kindness, gentleness, and self-control. Heal my heart, mind, body and soul.

In the name of Jesus I pray,

AMEN

# TRAUMA

Heavenly Father, I come broken and tired of the pain that I acquired from traumatic experiences in my childhood, youth, teenage years or adult life. Lord, remove every demonic spirit that entered my life due to trauma *(like: unbelief, mocking, addictions, pride, rebellion, anger, bitterness, violence, depression, grief, shame, unworthiness, failure, infirmities, control, fears, sexual sins, occult practices, abandonment, rejection, anxiety, deception, mental problems, family patterns, family curses and abortions)*. Lord, close every demonic door which was opened due to emotional, physical, mental, sexual, spiritual, or verbal abuse by *(name person: boyfriend, mother, father, uncle, friends pastor, church family, children, teacher, police officer, or boss)*.

The trauma caused by accidents (like: car, falls, death) that have imprisoned my mind, body and soul must leave. The trauma caused by violence – robbery, shootings, and murder must also flee in the name of Jesus. I bind and cast out every spirit of darkness that has entered my life through trauma. You have no authority here and you must leave now. Lord, fill those places which have been swept clean with your love, joy, peace, patience, self-control, gentleness, goodness, and faithfulness.

I call back every shattered piece of my soul. Put me back together again and make me whole, Father, by your grace and your mercy. Lord, I receive your healing, encouragement and comfort. Use me to comfort others who have been traumatized. Show me how to use my spiritual gifts to build people up.

*"Who comforteth us in all our tribulation, that we may be able to comfort them which are in any trouble, by the*

> *comfort wherewith we ourselves are comforted of God." 2*
> *Corinthians 1:4*

Use the word of my testimony and the ministry of love to bless those around me. I surrender my heart, mind, body, and soul. I commit myself to being your servant.

In the precious name of Jesus I pray,

AMEN

# UNBELIEF

Lord God, I confess the sin of doubt and unbelief. Lord, unbelief has hindered my relationship with you. Your word says faith pleases you so I ask that you would remove the spirit of unbelief from my heart, mind, body and soul.

*"Jesus said unto him, If thou canst believe, all things are possible to him that believeth. And straightway the father of the child cried out, and said with tears, Lord, I believe; help thou mine unbelief." Mark 9:23-24*

Lord, heal me of the negative life experiences that have discouraged me. I confess judging you for not answering my prayers in my timing or in my way. Forgive me, Father you are a good God and are working everything out for my good. I choose to believe and trust you.

By the power of the Holy Spirit I bind and cast out every evil spirit that has attached itself to me and caused confusion, double mindedness, doubt, fear, mistrust, skepticism, suspicion and uncertainty. You must go now.

Lord, fill me with your Holy Spirit and the fruit of the Spirit. I receive your wisdom, knowledge, understanding, revelation, and directions for my life. In the name of Jesus I pray, AMEN

# UNMOTIVATED

Heavenly Father, I have allowed the spirit of apathy and lack of motivation to come into my life through being rejected, discouraged, mocked, shamed, embarrassed, lied to, cheated, tricked, denied, and deceived. I have procrastinated and been irresponsible, lazy, and undisciplined. Father God, I confess my sin. I ask that you would break off each and every demonic spirit that has attached itself to my life. I bind the strong man that would cause me not to be diligent or motivated, I loose the purpose and plan of God in my life. Father, I lean not to my own understanding and I acknowledge you in all my ways, now direct my path.

*"I can do all things through Christ which strengtheneth me." Philippians 4:13*

Lord, I believe I can do all things through Christ, who strengthens me. No weapon formed against me shall prosper. Lord, show me how to take control of negative thoughts so I may clearly discern what you want me to do.

Heavenly Father, I thank you for motivation being restored. I can work hard unto you regardless of what man thinks of me. I will walk in the good works you have prepared for me to walk in. Not my will, but thy will be done.

In the name of Jesus I pray,
AMEN

# UNWORTHINESS

Father in Heaven, I feel worthless and unworthy. My past is filled with the sins I have committed and the sins that have been committed against me resulting in feelings of inadequacy, inferiority, insecurity, self-accusation, self-condemnation, self-hatred, and self-punishment. Today I ask for deliverance, healing and freedom.

I take authority over the spirits of darkness that have attached themselves to my mind, emotions, and body. In the name of Jesus, I bind and cast them out. I loose the peace, joy and righteousness of the Holy Ghost to rule and reign in my heart and my mind.

For the sins I have committed which have opened the door to the demonic, I repent. I confess the sins of thought, word or deed *(like: seducing, prostituting, making blue movies, exposing myself, lying, stealing, cheating, taking your Holy name in vain, not honoring the day of rest, disobeyed and disrespected my mother and father, adultery, giving false testimony, drug and alcohol use, and suicide attempts.)* Please forgive me, Lord.

I choose to forgive those who have sinned against me (name them) for spreading rumors about me, raping me, molesting me, abusing me, rejecting me, torturing me, discouraging me, mistreating me, entrapping me, betraying me, or casting spells on me. Lord, I forgive.

I surrender my emotions, heart, mind, body and soul to you, Lord Jesus. I ask you to continue the good work you are doing in my life. Lift up my head and allow me to feel your loving spirit.

> *"Being confident of this very thing, that he which hath begun a good work in you will perform it until the day of Jesus Christ." Philippians 1:6*

Surround me with a shield of protection and assign your angels to protect me from danger. Lord, make me more like you. I desire to know you better. Correct me when I get off of your path. I thank you for your forgiveness, you have made me worthy. Thank you for turning my life around and giving me your precious son, Jesus Christ, who died for my sins.

In the name of Jesus I pray,
AMEN

# VICTIM TO VICTOR

Lord Jesus, I thank you for your mercy which has kept me from dying as a victim of abuse, betrayal, deportation, imprisonment, suicide, addiction, helplessness, hopelessness, trauma, unfaithfulness, violence, drug wars or poverty. In the name of Jesus, I close the doors which opened my life up to the demonic *(like: being in a gang, selling drugs, ungodly soul ties, disloyal friends, abandonment by friends and family or emotional, physical, mental, sexual, spiritual or verbal abuse)*. I rebuke and command every ungodly spirit to leave my life, be cast down in the name of Jesus. Free my mind, Lord. Free my heart, my body and soul from ungodly acts and thoughts.

*"But thanks be to God, which giveth us the victory through our Lord Jesus Christ." 1 Corinthians 15:57*

I am no longer the victim of crime and abuse. I am victorious. Feelings of unworthiness, shame, grief, depression, bitterness, anger, rebellion, apathy, rejection, anxiety, and fear are replaced by the fruit of the Spirit – love, joy, peace, longsuffering, gentleness, goodness, faith, meekness, temperance. There is no law against walking after the Spirit. Old sinful patterns, involvements, and activities must all go from my life. In the name of Jesus I pray, AMEN

# VIOLENCE

Heavenly Father, I have sinned and fallen short of your glory through violence toward *(name: my mother, father, sister, brother, children, spouse, friends, peers, church family, teachers, boss, neighbor or police officer).* I ask that you forgive me and help me to turn from my angry and violent behavior. In the name of Jesus, I bind and cast out all arguing, bickering, cursing, feuding, mocking, contention, quarreling, fighting, conflict, discord, and turmoil. I loose the peace of God. Demonic spirits which have attached themselves to me because of abuse, cruelty, death, destruction, hate, murder, abortion, retaliation, strife, torture, unbelief, addictions, pride, or rebellion must go. Satan, I rebuke you in the name of Jesus.

All bitterness, depression, trauma, grief, shame, unworthiness, resentment, unforgiveness, abandonment, rejection, anxiety, deception, mental problems, infirmities, control, fears, occult practices, sexual sins, Jezebel syndromes, and cutting tongue must go too. Satan, the Lord rebukes you.

I command co-dependency, tribalism, idolatry, witchcraft, bloody warrior syndrome, and slave mentality to leave now in the name of Jesus. Holy Spirit, fill me with your love, peace, grace and mercy. Give me joy and help me walk after the Spirit and not after my flesh. Keep me on your path.

*"And that ye put on the new man, which after God is created in righteousness and true holiness." Ephesians 4:24*

Show me how to make restitution for the wrongs I have done to others. Heal the individuals and families that have been hurt by my violent behavior. Bless them today.

In the name of Jesus,
AMEN

# THE BEGINNING OF A WOMAN GLOBAL MINISTRY

The Vision: Do what Jesus did, The Great Commission, Saving souls and changing lives.

The Purpose: To be a vessel of the fruit of the spirit – love, peace, joy, patience, kindness, goodness, faithfulness, gentleness and self-control. Galatians 5:22, 23

The Goal: Reach the unreachable. Touch the untouchable. Go where some dare not go. Tread in places without a pass. Be a light in darkness. Do the unthinkable, accomplish the impossible and find the lost ones. (Yolanda Adams)

Mission Statement: We are dedicated to providing access to knowledge and resources, promoting lasting social and economic change, removing barriers and empowering individuals who are socially and economically disadvantaged in the Phoenix area and globally.

This ministry puts on the helmet of salvation, the breastplate of righteousness, shield of faith, the sword of the Spirit (the word of God), the belt of truth, and the foot gear ready to spread the good news. We put it on every minute, every hour and every day in the name of Jesus. This ministry is ready for the war. Are you ready for the war?

THE BEGINNING OF A WOMAN GLOBAL MINISTRY
P.O. Box 56163
Phoenix, Arizona 85079
602-326-6565

*Let the pastors bless His people. Let the church bless its leaders. Let the praise team and the choir bless the Lord. Let the parents bless the children. Let the schools bless the students. Let the missionary bless the world.*

*"Let every thing that hath breath praise the LORD. Praise ye the LORD." Psalm 150:6*

My Spiritual Growth Journal

30 Days of Healing, with Inspirational Scriptures
As you read the prayers daily journal
the manifestations of God's healing and delivering powers.

# My Spiritual Growth Journal

## 30 Days of Healing, with Inspirational Scriptures

*"Write my answer in large, clear letters on a tablet, so that a runner can read it and tell everyone else." ~ Hab. 2:2 ~*

# Journaling:

Why should I use a journal?

The purpose of a journal is to write down ideas, thoughts, experiences, visions and goals. A journal can also be used to record miracles, signs and wonders. (Heb. 2:4)

What should I write in my journal?

- Write down notes as you do your daily devotion.
- Journal every day.
- Write down revelation knowledge.
- The Holy Spirit might put a song, a prayer, a sermon or the name of your husband on your heart.
- Journaling can also be used as your witnessing tool.
- Record addresses, phone numbers and names of those who have come to Christ and are in need of Bible literature or other needs.
- Write down Bible verses or inspirational notes/phrases. Include how the phrases and/or Bible verses pertain to you.
- Write down what is happening in your life and how your thoughts daily.
- Keep track of any changes you go through during your healing and deliverance period.

# Day 1

Date: _____

| |
| --- |
| |
| |
| |
| |
| |
| |
| |
| |
| |
| |
| |
| |
| |
| |
| |
| |
| |
| |
| |
| |

# Day 2

Date:_____

> With this news, strengthen those who have tired hands, and encourage those who have weak knees. Say to those who are afraid, Be strong, and do not fear, for your God is coming to destroy your enemies. He is coming to save you." ~ Isa.35:3-4 ~

# Day 3

Date:_____

# Day 4

Date: _____

# Day 5

Date: _____

# Day 6

Date:_____

# Day 7

Date: _____

# Day 8

Date:_____

And God has actually given us
his Spirit (not the world's spirit)
so we can know the wonderful
things God has freely given us.
~ 1 Cor. 2:12 ~

# Day 9

Date:_____

# Day 10

Date:_____

# Day 11

Date:_____

For God has not given us a spirit
of fear and timidity, but of power,
love, and self-discipline.
~ 2 Tim. 1:7 ~

# Day 12

Date:_____

# Day 13

Date:_____

## Day 14

Date:_____

> O LORD, you alone can heal me;
> you alone can save. My praises
> are for you alone! ~ Jer. 17:14~

# Day 15

Date:_____

# Day 16

Date:_____

# Day 17

Date:_____

O LORD my God, I cried out to you
for help, and you restored my health.
~ Ps. 30:2 ~

# Day 18

*Date:* _____

# Day 19

Date:_____

# Day 20

Date: _____

# Day 21

Date:_____

# Day 22

Date:_____

# Day 23

Date:_____

> Love is patient and kind. Love is not jealous or boastful or proud 5or rude. Love does not demand its own way. Love is not irritable, and it keeps no record of when it has been wronged. 6It is never glad about injustice but rejoices whenever the truth wins out. 7Love never gives up, never loses faith, is always hopeful, and endures through every circumstance. ~ 1 Cor. 13:4-7 ~

# Day 24

Date:_____

# Day 25

Date:_____

# Day 26

Date:_____

> Why am I discouraged? Why so sad? I will
> put my hope in God!
> I will praise him again--my
> Savior and my God!
> ~ Ps. 42:11 ~

# Day 27

Date:_____

# Day 28

Date:_____

# Day 29

Date:_____

> For I know the plans I have for you,"
> says the LORD. "They are plans for
> good and not for disaster, to give you
> a future and a hope. ~ Jer. 29:11 ~

# Day 30

Date:_____

Printed in the United States
By Bookmasters